Contents

Getting started...

Your checklist for a happy healthy pet

- [ ] Hutch/indoor cage & run
- [ ] Ceramic food bowl
- [ ] Water bottle
- [ ] Woodshavings
- [ ] Hay
- [ ] Rabbit nuggets
- [ ] Mineral stone
- [ ] Vitamin supplement
- [ ] Probiotic supplement
- [ ] Treats
- [ ] Toys with hideaway holes
- [ ] Bottle brush
- [ ] Brush/ comb
- [ ] Gnawing sticks
- [ ] Cage disinfectant

Useful books

- [√] Good Pet Guide: The Rabbit
- [ ] Pet Friendly: Rabbits

Introduction

1. Rabbit

Rabbits are one of the worlds favorite domestic animals and currently one of the most widely kept pets, only behind cats and dogs in popularity. The reason for this little animals popularity is primarily down to their charming nature, ease to keep and availability, not to mention the vast variety of breeds, colors and coats.

Keeping rabbits as pets is an enjoyable experience for both the owner and rabbit. They are social and friendly animals and will love the companionship that fellow rabbits, as well as an attentive owner can provide.

Feeding a rabbit is relatively cheap and housing is diverse, whether keeping inside or outside. With the availability of easy to clean, large indoor enclosures, rabbits are becoming more and more popular as indoor pets.

The rabbit family can be loosely broken down into 4 kinds: **giant**, **standard**, **dwarf** and **mini**, however there are many sub groups and family divides.

"Did you know that a group of rabbits is called a 'herd'?"

2. Origins & habitat

In the wild, the domestic rabbit, can be traced back to the *Mediterranean rabbit (Oryctahus cuniculus)* which was introduced into Europe at around 1066.

As legend has it, they were not called *'rabbits'* until the 1300s when the Norwegians presented Robert the Bruce *(a keen hunter)* with a stock of wild rabbits as a gift. The Norse word for Robert was *'Rabit',* hence they became known as *'Roberts',* or as we know them today, *'rabbits'.*

In the wild, rabbits live in deep burrows in and around rich grassy plains and mounds, where they can be seen sprinting and playing amongst the grains and grasses upon which they feed. They are social animals and live in large communities, where the burrows form large interconnected systems generally known as *'warrens'.*

Rabbits have been kept abroad for centuries as a source of fur and food, but in the 1800s breeders became interested in showing and breeding different kinds of rabbits for trade purposes, as well as to create pets for the wealthy.

Now the humble rabbit is one of the most popular domestic pets in the world and is owned and loved by all social groups, both young and old.

EUROPE

Top tips

Litter training

Rabbits are very easy to litter train because they nearly always use the same one or two corners of the hutch as a toilet.

Simply place a rabbit suitable *'corner loo'* in the corner of the hutch that they use the most when you clean them out. Put in a layer of fresh hay and shavings plus the soiled litter from the corner you are putting the tray in. They will usually start to use the litter in the tray straight away. Then simply clean the tray out every two days, always putting a little of the soiled litter back in until they use it as habit.

3. Life span

Rabbits normally live between 5-8 years, but this can vary and is often extended by neutering.

Age isn't really an important factor when buying a rabbit as a pet. Your new pet should be adopted after the age of 8 weeks. At this age a rabbit would have been weaned off the mother and be readily eating solid foods.

Perfect pet?

4. Great pets

Rabbits enjoy exploring their environments. They are generally happy, inquisitive, lively and highly adaptable little pets.

This is why the rabbit is one of the most popular pets in so many countries. Rabbits are active most of the time, but they tend to be more active towards the evening time.

Rabbits are sociable animals and enjoy the company and security of other rabbits, especially if the owner is away during the days or your rabbit is kept in an outdoor hutch. They are relatively easy to handle as they have strong robust bodies and enjoy the warmth of a good cuddle and groom. With time and patience you will be able to feed them treats when holding them.

Rabbits world records

Oldest pet rabbit record :
16 yrs 2 mths *(Netherland dwarf 1990-06)*

Rabbit long jump world record :
118 inches (3 m)

Rabbit high jump world record :
39 inches (1 m)

Fun fact!

Rabbits by nature are very social creatures and can be kept together, provided they are bought at the same time. Once they reach adolescence they should be **neutered** or **spayed**, or you may end up with more pets than you want. This will reduce the possibilities of fighting.

5. One or more?

Rabbits become quite lonely on their own which can lead to health and behavioral problems. Keeping a male/ female pair is the easiest, although both should be neutered or you may end up with more pets than you wanted!

In the wild, rabbits live in close family colonies. When they are kept as pets their instincts are still much the same, so keeping several rabbits (of the same sex) ensures that their living conditions are as natural as possible.

You should not deprive your pet from the company of other rabbits if you feel they would like a companion, but indoor rabbits do tend to cope well on their own *(so long as they are in contact with you often)*. If you do choose to keep your rabbit outside then a friend for them would be well advised, as a pair of rabbits can cope with colder weather more easily as they will huddle together sharing body heat, whereas a lone rabbit could suffer from exposure *(which can be fatal)*. To further prevent the chances of exposure you should make sure that the hutch always has sufficient dry bedding and that the hutch is free from drafts *(see p8 'Hutch Huggers')*.

You can keep **does** *(female rabbits)* together with little problems, though spaying is advised for both health and temperament reasons. However, bucks *(male rabbits)* are slightly different. Adult males may fight with each other if they have not been brought up together from a young age, and even then, it isn't advisable that you keep more than two together, as this will certainly cause problems. Again, neutering is advised as this can help with territorial problems and also reduce urine odor.

Varieties

There are many breeds/ varieties of rabbit available, so to list all of them would take a whole volume.

Below is a list of the most common rabbits you will find:

6. Dutch

A very popular breed of rabbit. They have a gentle nature and are not very big, weighing no more than 5.5 lb (2.5 kg) at adulthood. A *dutch* rabbit is available in black, blue, fawn and occasionally with yellow markings. They have a bright white band running around their body, white paws and a white flash running down their nose.

7. English

One of the oldest breeds available today having been bred since the 1800s. The adult weight of an *English* rabbit is around 5.5- 6.6 lb (2.5- 3 kg) when fully grown. The ears are large and stand up proudly, moving to focus in on interesting sounds. The coat is distinguished by a black line that runs the length of the spine, black ringed eyes, black spots and a black patch on the nose *(the butterfly marking, as it is referred to)* while the rest of the body is bright white.

8. Netherland Dwarf

The most commonly found dwarf rabbit in pet shops. Adults should weigh around 2.2 lb (2 kg). They have short pointed ears around 2 inches (5 cm) in length and are available in a number of colors and patterns. They have a life expectancy of more than 8 years. Quite mischievous in character, they can be a little feisty for young children.

9. Dwarf Lop

Despite the name, this is not a dwarfed rabbit. The name is somewhat misleading because these rabbits can still reach an impressive 6.0 lb (2.7 kg) in weight. They are generally good natured, especially when spayed/ neutered. The coat is quite thick and will require grooming several times a week.

10. Hotot *(pronounced O- toe)*

This is one of the most endearing rabbits. The adult weight is around 3.3 lb (1.5 kg) with short pointed ears of around 3 inches (7.5 cm) high. The most recognizable feature of this little rabbit is their black rings that shade their eyes.

Top tips

Mini Lop

A miniature variety of the standard lop rabbit and *dwarf lop*.

Polish Rabbit

This small, intelligent rabbit is often quite difficult to handle. They require patience and regular contact to become calm in your presence. They are generally healthy rabbits.

Harlequin

A beautifully marked breed. They have an orange coat with black bands and black mottles. Sometimes half of the head and face is black while the other side is orange. The underbelly is usually a lighter tone of orange, or even yellow white with mottled feet.

Lion Head

This rabbit is a very beautiful rabbit indeed. It has a body of roughly the same size as that of the *Netherland Dwarf*, however, with a stunning main of hair behind the head and jaw which may also extend along the lower body when young.

Your rabbit

11. Male or female?

Female rabbits are called *'does'* and male rabbits are called *'bucks'.* While the personalities of male and females do not differ greatly there are certain things to consider when purchasing your rabbit and which sex you choose.

Both males and females should be *neutered*. The males *(for personality reasons)* as when they reach around 4 months of age they can become temperamental as testosterone develops and also to lessen the smell of their urine. With females, it is less to do with personality, and more to do with health reasons. If you do not plan to let your female mate by 6 to 8 months of age she should be *spayed*, as *does* can develop ovarian cysts or at worst certain cancers as a result of not being spayed or mated. The two pictures and instructions below should help when you are sexing your rabbits:

Top tips

Any doubts?

Even pet shop owners can make mistakes with the sex of rabbits as they are incredibly difficult to sex at an early age because of the similarities of the genitalia, so it is usually a good idea to double check before purchasing.

✔

Male *(bucks)*   Female *(does)*

The left shows the buck *(male)* while the right shows the doe. Notice that the bucks' genitals are completely retractable only leaving a raised ring *(this is clearly visible by the time the buck reaches maturity at around 6 weeks)*; also notice the end of the penis has a small hole, creating a tube.

The female *(doe)* has a similar looking tube, though the tube has a slightly larger hole that runs a little down the middle of the tube.

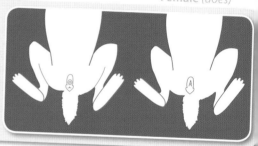

Important!
Spaying the female should be performed no earlier than 5 months old as the operation is far more intrusive than the males neutering.

THE RABBIT 6

12. **Choosing your rabbit**

Ensure that the pet you choose is active and interested in its surroundings, has a glossy coat, clean ears, bright eyes, and a well rounded body free of bumps or swellings.
Below are a few things to consider when choosing your rabbit:-

→ Mouth

A rabbits' mouth should have no signs of dribbling or scabbing at the corners *(this can be a sign of a fungal infection).*

→ Eyes

Should be bright and alert with no sign of discharge or cloudiness. If they look dull it could be a sign of a more serious health issue, check regularly for foreign bodies.

→ Ears

The ears should be free from hair loss and scabs on both the inside and out. A lop eared breed can suffer from other issues, such as waxy build ups and foreign bodies. A small amount of wax in the ear is normal but if more than this is present it should be cleaned out.

→ Teeth

A rabbits' teeth constantly grow as they are what are called *'open rooted.'* One tooth problem to look for when choosing your new pet is the *'splaying'* of the top front teeth. Or a condition called *'malocclusion,'* which is when the top and bottom teeth do not align correctly, this condition will be present from birth.

→ Nose

Make sure the nose is clean; there shouldn't be any mucus in or around the nose. Rabbits naturally carry a condition called *'pasteurella'* sometimes just called *'the snuffles,'* if the rabbit you are looking at has wet front feet *'hankies'* It may be a sign that the rabbit has the snuffles, usually brought on by stress, poor hygiene or if the rabbit is feeling run down.

→ Tail

One of the most endearing features of the rabbit is the *'flash'* tail. This should be clean and free from dried faecal matter.

→ Paws

The front paws should be free from stickiness *(this could be a sign of illness, as they wipe their nose and eyes on their front paws and ankles 'hankies')* All the paw bottoms have hair so it is not reasonable to expect them to be immaculate, although they shouldn't be very dirty and covered in faecal matter.

→ Hair

If the hair around the rabbits' rump and tail is matted, it could mean the rabbit is suffering from **diarrhoea** or at worse, *'bloat' (see p13).* It should have a glossy but not greasy coat with no bald patches.

→ Attitude/ personality

They should show an alert posture or a relaxed flattened posture, have a healthy appetite and sharp, lively reactions *(a lethargic, hunched unkempt rabbit is one that isn't in peak condition).*

It is a common view that a pet that runs to you wanting attention is the one that you should have. But with rabbits they tend to bolt quickly and hide, showing that it has healthy, spritely nervous system that is working well.

Housing rabbits

13. Outdoors

If an outdoor hutch is used, extra insulation is usually needed in colder months as rabbits can suffer from chills and drafts. Hideaways and extra hay and straw bedding is essential especially in winter.

The hutch should be kept shaded and out of direct drafts. A shed, walled areas or porch will suffice. By doing this, the hutch is kept out of the elements and will minimize risk to your pets' health. There should always be a secure bedding area in the hutch that contains warm, dry bedding, this area should be draft free, but still, provide ventilation.

If you can't keep your hutch out of the elements then you must ensure that the hutch is properly insulated against wind, rain and damp. You can purchase a *'Hutch Hugger'* which will protect the hutch and your rabbit against bad weather *(available from most pet stores)*. You should ensure that your rabbits' home is a safe environment for your pet, safe from animals getting in as well as preventing your rabbit escaping.

Ideally, you need to give your rabbit room to run, play and stand on its back legs. A size of 4' x 10' x 2½' high (120cm x 300cm x 75cm high) is recommended for most rabbits.

14. Indoors

Rabbits are comfortable in the same temperature range as humans, so indoor housing is not an issue, though be careful if you then decide to put them in an outdoor hutch, as the sudden change in temperature can cause illness.

There are a few considerations when keeping indoors, though keeping your pets indoors will make bonding with your pet easier as you will find that your pet will be tamer as a result.

Even rabbits that are housed in outdoor hutches need to come indoors from time to time. When the weather outside means that your outdoor run or grazing area cannot be used, it is still important that your rabbits can exercise, they require daily exercise and leaving them locked up for long periods is not advised. They will be quite happy exploring inside the home. Just ensure that all cables are out of reach, that other animals are supervised and it has a suitable bolt hole to hide in should it get scared *(upturned cardboard boxes make good little hidey holes)*.

15. Introducing the hutch

You should be prepared and have your new pets hutch set up fully before their arrival, preferably have it set up for a day before.

Let them roam freely to begin with to explore their new surroundings. Try not to pick your new pet up for a few days to let them get accustomed to their new home and you. Speak softly to your rabbit and use their name frequently.

Once they are used to their new home, be careful to acclimatize them to human contact slowly. Start by stroking your rabbit with one finger while they are roaming and eating in their run. Next, start using the full hand, then occasionally lifting it *(handling p18)*, until such a time as it is comfortable with you and with being held.

16. Outdoor runs & enclosures

Outside of the colder months your rabbit may have a wire mesh enclosure that is often referred to as a run attached to it via a ramp so that the hutch space can be extended out onto a lawn.

This gives your rabbit more chance to explore their surroundings and make the most of the warmth and soft summer breezes. Rabbits are grazers so act as great lawn mowers and they will ensure that your garden is kept trim. However, at night your pet should always be shut into the main hutch area with a catch or bolt, especially if there is a danger of attack from animals.

Hidey holes

Rabbits love hidey holes and will actively seek them out and plan escape routes to them when wandering around. This type of hiding place simulates the same feeling of security that they would have in their wild habitats.

All rabbits should have a structure in their cage or hutch to hide in *(this helps to satisfy their instinct to flee when they feel threatened)*, either a wooden hidey hole or woven bedding area will provide enough of a snug environment to make them feel safe. These are also used to chew on *(Rabbits need to chew regularly to keep their teeth worn down)*.

1. Two Storey Rabbit hutch.
2. Rabbit friendly hutch.
3. Rabbit friendly hidey hole.
4. Rabbit friendly enclosure/ run.

4.

Young Children
Young children must always be supervised when with their rabbits.

Rabbit food guide

17. Food glorious food

Every rabbit will have different likes and dislikes and it is up to you find foods that your pets likes as well as having a positive effect on its health.

It is important to know what you can and cannot feed your pet to avoid harming it and to help make sure your pet is receiving all the nutrients that they need to stay healthy. In their natural environment their diet would mainly consist of grasses and seeds, therefore in captivity you should simulate this as close as possible.

Rabbits like all herbivores require the long indigestible fiber in grass and hay for their unique digestive system; it also helps to keep their teeth under control and at the correct length.

They should have an unlimited supply of hay and can live quite happily on a diet of good quality hay, pure dried grass, wild plants, herbs and vegetables. You should always try to provide a staple diet for your pet and plenty of fresh water. Do not use a water bowl though as this will become soiled and unsanitary. Instead, use a specially design small animal water bottle. (See page 11).

1.

18. Fresh foods

Good foods for your rabbit include:
Cauliflower leaves (but not the white 'flower') | broccoli florets | purple sprouting broccoli | carrots | parsnips | sweetcorn | cucumber | parsley | spring greens | basil | spinach | apple

Good wild plants include:
Golden rod | cleavers | yarrow | dandelion (given sparingly as dandelion is a diuretic) | mallow | shepherds purse

Bad foods/ plants:-
Potato | rhubarb | tomato leaves | daffodil | tulip | cabbage (can cause bloat) and lily of the valley | lettuce

2.   3.

19. Pellets

There are specially made pellets just for rabbits that can be the mainstay of a healthy rabbits' diet.

When used in conjunction with the fresh foods as listed opposite, they can be used to good effect to provide a well balanced nutritious diet. Another benefit with pellet food is that it restricts your rabbit from selective feeding and also aids in tooth maintenance.

4.

5.

6.

Top tips

Rodents

Rabbits are not Rodents, they are Lagomorphs.

The difference between most rodents and *Lagomorpha* is that they are strict vegetarians and cannot stomach animal derived produce such as milk, cheese and yogurt as they are lactose intolerant, though as a winter protein in the wild they may eat carrion. They also have different tooth arrangements, however their teeth do continue to grow like those of rodents.

20. Hay/ straw

Rabbits should always have access to a constant supply of hay.

Grass hay such as *oat, timothy* or *meadow hay* is essential to their digestion and is a large percentage of what they eat. You should supplement this with any good rabbit feed and fresh vegetables *(only give to a rabbit around 4 months old and then only in small doses until they are used to it)* for a well rounded healthy diet. It is important that any hay you use is dry, clean and mould free.

Straw is only used as a bedding material and as extra bedding in the winter. A good barley straw is best because it has a soft texture.

21. Treats

Special treats include apple and fruit woods.

Fresh fruits and vegetables such as strawberries and carrots are eagerly enjoyed, especially the green carrot tops. You can also buy many treats from you local pet shop such as healthy natural dried herbs and hanging sticks.

Important!
Do not give your rabbit commercial treats that contain any sugar, salt or dairy.

7.

22. Water

The amount of water a rabbit needs will vary.

It is always advisable that you have a constant supply of water within easy reach of your rabbit, whether it's kept in the house, cage or grazing enclosure. Make sure you change the water and clean the bottle regularly. Bowls are not recommended as they quickly become soiled and unhealthy for your pet to drink from.

8.

1. Rabbit treat.
2. Broccoli.
3. Potato.
4. Rabbit muesli.
5. Rabbit chocolate drops.
6. Rabbit friendly wood mix.
7. Carrots.
8. Water bottle.

Play time

23. Exercise

Your rabbits will benefit greatly from being kept fit and healthy. Well exercised rabbits will live longer and have fewer health problems.

Rabbits can experience health problems that arise from being overweight. They will have higher tendencies for heart disease, diabetes, bladder infections, respiratory problems and joint conditions.

A large hutch with enough room to play and exercise can help keep your pet to keep in shape and ensure that they live a richer, healthier life. Ensure that the hutch you choose has lots of shade or cover for your rabbits to hide in when frightened or seeking security.

Rabbits do not need the same exercise provisions as other small animals such as hamsters and gerbils, they will generally be happy enough to run around in a large enclosure with one or two simple toys for the times when they are most active. If you don't give your rabbit enough things to entertain itself, it will be inactive and as a result, bored and unhappy.

An active pet is a happy pet!

Top tips

Curiousity

Rabbits are by nature incredibly curious little creatures.

It is always a good idea to hide treats for them inside willow toys or make a Christmas cracker type toys by placing a treat inside a kitchen roll tube and twisting the ends closed. This will encourage your pet to wear down their teeth by gnawing through the cardboard, whilst entertaining them by trying to retrieve the treat.

24. Play

Rabbits are quite active and playful little animals who love to engage themselves in games, either on their own or with one of their companions.

They often play alone and will happily amuse themselves with simple toys *(see below)*, but they especially love to play with one another. Rabbits love to tear up and toss around paper bags, finding them a great deal of fun to play with and chew on.

25. Accessories

Different rabbits like different toys, so while some will love one toy, another will simply ignore it.

It is good to experiment and give them a variety of different toys, most of which they will ignore, but persist until you find something that entertains your particular pet. Usually the simpler the toy the better.

Some rabbit favorites are:

A toilet paper tube | a medium sized cardboard box | willow balls | plastic animal ball with bell | hanging fruit wood toys | a straw basket | wood blocks | branches.

1. Wooden toy
2. Rabbit fun tree
3. Willow ball
4. Cardboard tube

1.

2.

3.

4.

Important!
Change the toys, houses, and the locations frequently to keep things fresh and interesting for your pet.

Rabbit grooming

26. Grooming

Grooming is a daily requirement. It is important that you take good care of your pet to ensure that it is clean and healthy, especially the long haired and rex varieties.

Rabbits molt constantly because of temperature changes throughout the year and through grooming. Regular brushing ensures that their coat is always at its best.

Rabbits love to groom themselves. However, they will still appreciate regular grooming from you. As well as being beneficial to your pet, this will also help you to bond with your pet.

1.

It is important that the rough/ long haired varieties of rabbits are brushed regularly and their hair is kept in a good condition. They are prone to their hair becoming matted and knotted and this can become quite unpleasant and painful for your pet if left unchecked. With long haired breeds it is best to groom them daily to prevent this. It will also give you an ideal opportunity to check your rabbit for anything out of the ordinary that could indicate a health issue. If you are unsure of anything that you find, consult your vet.

To groom your rabbit you will need a:

Brush: Soft pin brush is best *(pictured above)*
Comb: A flea comb is best for smooth short coated varieties, although you may need a wider toothed barber comb for a longer haired variety.
Nail trimmer: Guillotine type or human kind can work as well.

27. Trimming nails

We recommend you take your rabbit to the veterinarian for nail trimming.

However, in time and with the relative experience you may find that you can do it yourself. Although, it is advised that you first speak to a veterinary surgeon who can guide you through the technique of rabbit nail trimming.

2.

It is important to note that there is a part within the nail called the *'quick,'* this vein is where the blood vessels and nerve endings are located. If you do accidently cut into the *quick* you will cause bleeding as well as considerable pain to you pet. The aim is to just clip the sharp tip of the nail without damaging the *quick*.

1. Rabbits friendly grooming kit.
2. Rabbit friendly nail trimmer.

Health

28. Good health

To ensure your rabbit remains in good health, make sure that their diet has an adequate intake of vitamins and minerals, through a fresh and high quality diet.

29. Wood gnaws

Wood gnaws are available in pet shops or you can provide your own by supplying the rabbit with a piece of unsprayed fruit branch or untreated *wood block* to gnaw on.

These will provide your pet with something on which to keep its teeth nice and trim. It would be a good idea to age the branches if you choose to use these, as the drying process is extremely important because some of these branches are poisonous when fresh.

30. Health checks

Here are a couple of easy health checks that you can do yourself whilst your pet is sitting on you lap.

Check through your pets coat by running the tip of your finger against the lay of the hair to see if there is any dry skin or bald spots which may be indicative of a fungal or parasitic skin condition.

Check that the teeth aren't broken or loose.

Checks to see if the nose is dry, eyes are bright and that the rabbit is lively and alert.

Top tips

Rabbit vision

Because of the position of a rabbit's eyes they can see almost 360 degrees around themselves, but they can see almost nothing in front of their noses.

This is because they are a prey animal in the wild and need to be able to see what is approaching them while they graze. So, it is always best to approach your rabbit from the front side so they can see you. If you approach them from behind they may see you as a threat and hide away.

Vaccinations!

All rabbits should be vaccinated against both Viral Haemorrhagic Disease (VHD/ RHVD/ RCD) and myxomatosis.

31. Health problems

➜➜ Constipation and diarrhoea

Take these very seriously, they can both be caused by a bad diet or illnesses like *bloat*. Consult a vet if you've any queries.

➜➜ Parasites

Scratching is a common symptom of a skin complaint often brought about by parasites like *lice, mites* and *fleas*. Rabbits are usually free from parasites but should your pet get an infestation, treat with a specialized medicated shampoo, mild insecticide powder or small animal *Spot On* drop. If you have any queries, seek veterinary advice. The most common type of parasite is the *'Seasonal static hay mite'* this particular mite is very difficult to see and only causes a problem when the infestation becomes too large and your rabbit scratches continuously. At the first sign of any kind of parasite, immediate treatment is the most effective course of action.

➜➜ Respiratory infections

Rabbits are not to prone to respiratory infections, but if they do contract one they will usually have very similar symptoms to the human common cold. However, it can be have a more serious impact on rabbits and should not be left untreated as it can lead to pneumonia. Keep out of damp environments and if the symptoms continue, consult your veterinary for further advice.

➜➜ Bloat

There are two kinds, *wet bloat* and *gaseous bloat*. It can be caused by stress, as a secondary infection or as a result of a diet change. The obvious signs of both bloats are a swollen hard stomach, lack of appetite, lethargy and dehydration. With wet bloat, a clear mucus usually runs from the anus when picked up or if the stomach is lightly compressed, and very wet passing's before constipation sets in. Seek advice from a veterinary as soon as possible if you suspect bloat as it can be fatal.

➜➜ Eye injuries

These are very common in rabbits and indeed all hutched animals. Usually, caused by hay or straw poking into their eyes. A saline wash will flush the eye of any foreign bodies but consult your veterinarian if problems persist.

Top tips

➜➜ Teeth

The rabbits' teeth are very important and can suffer from over growth or impaction due to breed problems. One condition is called *'malocclusion'* which is a congenital condition where the roots impact into the jaw, and the top and bottom teeth are unable to meet, resulting in over growth. Unless pure breed, some rabbits suffer from a *burring* of the back teeth.

➜➜ Fly strike

Normally during the end of the summer months. It is caused by the blow fly laying eggs in feces-soiled fur. Within 24 hrs, larvae hatch out and eat their way into the rabbits rectum. You should check your pet daily to ensure their coat is free from feces.

➜➜ Worms

Rabbits are affected by both *roundworms* and *tapeworms*. Symptoms include a distended abdomen, poor coat and worms in the feces.

Other things to look out for are: lethargy, a dull or uneven coat, and a crouching posture. *If you think your rabbit is unwell, take your pet to a qualified vet.*

✔

Cage care

32. Home sweet home

A covering is required for the floor of the cage to provide a soft, comfortable surface for the rabbit as well as soaking up urine. The most common type of floor covering available is wood shavings. Fine sawdust should be avoided as this can cause irritation to the eyes and to the lungs.

Cedar wood shavings *(usually distinguished by a red tint)* should not be used as the *phenols* they contain can cause severe irritations in rabbits. Although pine is also a softwood, **pine wood shavings** cause less problems than cedar and **kiln dried pine** can be used without problems.

You should steer clear of any scented shavings such as lemon and lavender as these can cause irritation to your pet. Corn cob bedding is not generally recommended either. It has a tendency to mould, and rabbits have been known to eat it and it can then swell when wet inside the stomach.

Shavings from hardwoods like aspen or small animal litter made from wood pulp are the safest forms of floor covering to use.

33. Cage cleaning

Rabbits themselves have a sweet smell, however even a sweet smelling pets' cage will smell if it isn't cleaned for an extended period. Urine soaked bedding, feces and decaying vegetable matter all make your pets' hutch an unpleasant place to live and encourage flies and other pests to take hold.

→ Once a day you should remove all droppings.

→ Check that the bedding and cage litter is dry *(as damp conditions are bad for rabbits).*

→ Tidy the sleeping area and ensure that they have fresh clean water and the bottle is free of algae *(use a mild animal safe detergent weekly to clean the bottle, rinse thoroughly and replace with fresh water in the hutch).*

→ Once a week, clean the whole hutch using a sturdy brush and good animal-friendly cleaning disinfectant *(wait until the inside of the hutch is dry before replacing the litter and bedding and putting your pets back in).*

Top tips

Timothy hay, alfalfa hay & meadow hay

Rabbits need roughage in the form of either of these hays.

They can be obtained from any local pet shop. Do not buy hay that is damp as this can be moldy and dangerous for your pet. Keep it stored in a dry, cool place.

Timothy or **standard meadow** hays are the favored choices as **alfalfa** hay is already included in rabbit pellets and can be a contributing factor to some rabbits becoming overweight.

Important!

Remove your rabbits and make sure you place them in a safe and secure place before you begin cleaning their hutch.

Handling rabbits

34. Gently does it

Rabbits are nervous animals to begin with, but they are also very simple animals to handle. However, to begin with they won't enjoy being lifted up at all. They will need to be taught gradually from a young age to tolerate being handled.

In the beginning get your pet used to you by feeding it bits of vegetable or fruit from your hand *(parsley is a favorite)* and talking softly to them, using their name frequently. In time it will become used to this and will let you stroke it whilst it is feeding. Don't worry if it does not become accustomed to this straight away, be patient and allow your pet to become comfortable with you. Once you have achieved this, you will be able to move on to the next stage.

When picking up a rabbit, approach them slowly, and only from the front side *(see Top tips p15)*. They are easily startled and are certain to run for cover if they feel like they are being stalked by a predator. Try to keep them calm throughout the whole process. Talk gently to your pet whilst gently stroking it.

Once you have gained their trust, place one hand firmly on its back *(not to firmly though as you don't want to damage their fragile bones and organs)* and place the remaining hand under their rump, just behind the front feet, then move your other hand to support its back end, tucking their feet under them and against your chest.

Bring it in close to your chest, continuing to support it using both hands, one supporting its back end and the other placed over the shoulders. Always lift your pet with smooth and gentle movements as not to scare it. If you are new to rabbits or have one that really struggles, then you should kneel down on the floor to lift them up, this will minimize the chance of any injury should your pet wriggle free from your grasp. They are fragile creatures and can suffer greatly if dropped, even if from a short height.

Did you know?

A rabbits tail is not just for decoration. It is white on the under side so they can warn other rabbits of danger at a distance by flicking it up.

35. Small children and safety

Children should be sat down *(preferably on the floor)*, when you pass the rabbit to them.

Teach them to be gentle and to only stroke the hair in the direction that it is growing.

When placing your pet back in the hutch, they can become quite excited, so be extra careful not to drop them. Try to release your hold on them only once they are safely on the floor of the hutch.

36. Stroking

If your rabbit does not want to be stroked, it will let you know by kicking free or spinning their body around and kick upwards, or pushing away the hand that strokes it.

When met with this response it is wise to honor your rabbits wishes and stop stroking it. It either means it doesn't like being stroked there or is bored of it. Ignoring this will only hinder your bonding process and could result in a light bite.

37. Vocalizations

Rabbits are rather quiet little characters, preferring body language and hind foot thumps to express themselves.

They do however make some noises such as *'loud snuffles'* if they are nervous and *'grunts'* if annoyed.

38. Sociable nature

Rabbits have a highly social nature and it is not recommended that you keep them as solitary pets.

Regardless of how much attention you give them, they will still suffer from loneliness, especially if there is no one in the house to fuss over them during the day.

Try to spend time with your pet whenever you can. Sitting with your pets in the garden as they play in their run from time to time is a good idea, however it is still recommended that you get another rabbit friend to keep them company if they are to be left for long periods.

Know your rabbit

39. Rabbit anatomy

The anatomy of a the humble rabbit is the result of millions of years of natural selection in nature. It has proven itself to be one of the most well evolved and resilient of all the *'hunted species'.*

Originally classified as rodents, it was decided in 1912 that rabbits, because of their extra set of front teeth *(positioned behind their first set of incisors),* were part of the mammal genus *'lagamorpha'.*

Rabbits are referred to as *Hind Gut* fermenters. Like all vegetarian animals, they rely on carefully balanced bacteria within their stomachs to break down their fiber heavy diet in order to extract the most nutrients from it. Your rabbit may not be able to extract all of the nutrients at once hence they practice a behavior called *'caprophagia'.* **Caprophagia** is the eating of sticky clumped faecal pellets called *'caecotrophs'.* This second passing contains the extra nutrients that the rabbit could not fully digest in the stomach upon first break down. Although this sounds unusual to us, it is very beneficial to your rabbit and common practice among the Lagamorpha species.

You will notice that a rabbit has, in proportion to their bodies, rather large back feet. This is because a rabbit is a flee animal and rely on their powerful rear legs and sturdy feet to propel them at fantastic speeds with amazing agility to avoid attackers. You will notice that when a rabbit becomes excited or is nervous of what they perceive as a threat, they thump their feet loudly. In the wild this thumping is use to warn other rabbits still in the warren of a threat above and to stay below.

Biggest rabbit

The worlds biggest rabbit is the German Giant and is a hutch busting 3 stone (19 kg) in weight and is nearly 3 ft (91 cm) in length!

✔

Important!

Because of the rabbits poor frontal vision, always approach your pet from the front side rather than head on.

40. Rabbit behavior

→ **Touching noses, nuzzling**

Greeting & acknowledgement. Reserved for familiar friends.

→ **Jumping**

Jumping straight up in the air and kicking out with the hind legs is a typical display of joy.

→ **Sitting up or standing with ears pointed forward**

Checking the surrounding area, inquisitiveness.

→ **Lowering the head drawing into themselves**

Fear, submission and can be seen as an offering of peace.

→ **Playing dead**

Playing dead often occurs when your rabbit is very relaxed, they literally drop on to one side and stretch out.

→ **Stretching the head forwards**

Watchful and alert, sniffing the air.

→ **Stress**

Rabbits, especially dwarf varieties are susceptible to stress much like humans, but unlike us, they have no way of changing their lives to make it better for themselves. Stress will impact on your pets' immune system and can adversely affect its ability to fight off infections.

Keep your rabbit away from extreme temperatures, out of noisy environments and away from intimidating animals/people. To relieve stress make sure your pet is well exercised and has plenty of interaction between yourself and their friends if housed together.

→ **Hair stripping**

A curious behavior where your rabbit may start to strip and clip the hair from its body and/or their cage mates, this is most commonly caused by boredom, brought on by inactivity and a lack of gnawing toys. It can also be a sign of mites or Illness.

→ **Boxing**

Rabbits are renowned for their boxing skills. A rabbit will lean back onto their hind legs and hold their front paws in a boxing position. They do this as part of play or to defend themselves from attack.

→ **Out-stretched**

An out-stretched posture is a sign of being relaxed.

→ **Retracting legs under body and backed up against a wall**

Helpless and scared, needing protection.

Breeding advice

41. Golden rules of breeding

The best advice is to leave breeding to the experts! Breeding should only be considered with careful thought and understanding for the offspring that will be produced.

It is important to know that your rabbits will reach sexual maturity very quickly indeed, so if you wish to avoid offspring, you must keep the male rabbits separated from the females unless neutered.

Where lop and dwarf rabbits are concerned you need to be especially careful as there is a risk of congenital teeth problems such as *impaction* and *splaying (see Top tips p16)*. So only breed with known healthy rabbits from different families.

42. Baby rabbits

Straight after birth, it is very important that you keep the male away from the female because he will mate with her immediately after birth and two pregnancies so close to one another can cause a massive strain on the doe.

The doe will not tolerate the bucks presence during pregnancy and will become quite aggressive toward him. It is wise to remove the male should this happen.

Do not interfere with the mother or her young as she may eat her babies if she feels threatened or if they carry your scent on them.

The gestation period for rabbits is 28- 31 days and the weaning period is 8 weeks, after this time the babies may be removed from the mother. The pups are born blind and hairless and rely totally on the mother for food, warmth and protection.

Top tips

Fastest rabbit

The fastest rabbit, the *Jack* rabbit can run at an amazing 45 mph (72 km/h). While the domestic standard sized rabbit can run at an impressive 25 mph (40 km/h)!

✔

"Did you know that my home in the wild is called a 'Warren'?"

43. Preparing the cage

If you have decided that you would like to breed your own rabbits you should prepare the cage with the little mother and babies in mind.

The mother should have plenty of hay and soft straw as she will use most of what is put in for her to create her birthing nest, she will also use her own hair to insulate the nest. Extra food and water should be available before and after the birth. Rabbits are kind and devoted mothers and will look after their young intently provided they are left alone.

44. Introductions

You may wish to mate your own rabbit with a friends rabbit or one purchased to begin your breeding program. Although rabbits are friendly and agreeable little creatures with their own kind, introductions can be difficult.

Females tend to take to a new friend easier than males, but any introduction must be done slowly and with care. One method is to place your new rabbit in a cage next to your existing pets and swap the bedding to and from the cages on a daily basis until they become familiar with each others scent. Next you allow them to run together in neutral surroundings for short periods at a time and then finally they can be placed together.

Signs to watch for when introducing are:

Stamping - this is a warning or a sign of excitement.

Scenting - both sexes may flick their rear ends and their tail to spray a heavy scented liquid at each other and around their territory.

Tail lifting - one rabbit will chase the other, lifting the others rump with their nose, the male will do this to the doe to see if she is receptive.

Vibrating - one rabbit may jump on top of the other and vibrate and scent them, this is to show the other who is boss and in charge.

You may see your rabbits boxing, this can be a serious sign of aggression if they are not familiar with each other so they must be separated at this point for their own safety. If this behavior goes on for more than 48 hours the introduction unfortunately may not work.

Top tips

Hutch size

Larger rabbits require larger hutches or cages.

Make sure that any hutch or cage you buy gives them enough height to stand on their back legs and hop at least three to four times in any direction to avoid them becoming bored or unable to investigate their home. If their home is too small they may become bored or develop *urine burn* on their feet and bellies from being stuck in the same spot for to long.

✔

Titles in series

Copyright © 2013 Magnet & Steel Ltd
Publisher: Magnet & Steel Ltd
Printed and bound in China by PRINTWORKS Int. Ltd.

Magnet & Steel Ltd
Unit 6
Vale Business Park,
Llandow, United Kingdom. CF71 7PF
sales@magnetsteel.com
www.magnetsteel.com